Leader's Guide
for group study of

PUTTING AWAY CHILDISH THINGS

DAVID A SEAMANDS

Leader's Guide prepared by
DUFFY ROBBINS

Ten Multiuse Transparency Masters (for visual aids) are included in a removable center section. Instructions for using them are on pages 5-6.

VICTOR

BOOKS a division of SP Publications, Inc.
WHEATON. ILLINOIS 60187

Offices also in
Whitby, Ontario, Canada
Amersham-on-the-Hill, Bucks, England

ISBN: 0-88207-423-7

General Preparation

Survey the entire *Text* and this *Leader's Guide*. *This is basic.* Underline important passages in the text and make notes as ideas come to you, before you forget them. Become familiar with the entire course, including all units in the *Guide* that you will be using in your study. A general knowledge of what is coming up later will enable you to conduct each session more effectively and to keep discussion relevant to the subject at hand. If questions are asked that will be considered later in the course, postpone discussion until that time.

Add to your teaching notes any material and ideas you think important or of special help to your class. As teacher, your enthusiasm for the subject and your personal interest in those you teach, will in large measure determine the interest and response of your class.

We recommend strongly that you plan to use teaching aids, even if you merely jot down a word or two on a chalkboard from time to time to impress a point on the class. When you ask for a number of answers to a question, as in brainstorming, always jot down each answer in capsule form, to keep all ideas before the group. If no chalkboard is available, use a magic marker on large sheets of newsprint over a suitable easel. A printer can supply such paper for you at modest cost.

Once you have decided what visual or audio aids you will use, make sure *all* the necessary equipment is on hand *before* classtime. If you use electrical equipment such as projector or recorder, make sure you have an extension cord available if needed. For chalkboards, have chalk and eraser. That's obvious, of course, but small details are easily forgotten.

Encourage class members to bring Bibles or New Testaments to class and use them. It is good to have several modern-speech translations on hand for purposes of comparison.

Getting Started Right

Start on time. This is especially important for the first session for two reasons. First, it will set the pattern for the rest of the course. If you begin the first lesson late, members will have less reason for being on time at the others. Those who are punctual will be robbed of time, and those who are habitually late will come still later next time. Second, the first session should begin promptly because getting acquainted, explaining the procedure, and introducing the textbook will shorten your study time as it is.

Begin with prayer, asking the Holy Spirit to open hearts and minds, to give understanding, and to apply the truths that are studied. The Holy Spirit is the great Teacher. No teaching, however orthodox and carefully presented, can be truly Christian or spiritual without His control.

Involve everyone. The suggested plans for each session provide a maximum of participation for members of your class. This is important because—

1. People are usually more interested if they take part.
2. People remember more of what they discuss together than they

do of what they are told by a lecturer.
3. People like to help arrive at conclusions and applications. They are more likely to act on truth if they apply it to themselves than if it is applied to them by someone else.

To promote relaxed involvement, you may find it wise to—
1. Have the class sit in a circle or semicircle. Some who are not used to this idea may feel uncomfortable at first, but the arrangement makes class members feel more at home. It will also make discussion easier and more relaxed.
2. Remain seated while you teach (unless the class numbers over 25).
3. Be relaxed in your own attitude and manner. Remember that the class is not "yours," but the Lord's, so don't get tense!
4. Use some means to get the class better acquainted, unless all are well-known to each other. At the first meeting or two each member could wear a large-lettered name tag. Each one might also briefly tell something about himself, and perhaps tell what, specifically, he expects to get from this study.

Adapting the Course
This material is designed for quarterly use on a weekly basis, but it may be readily adapted to different uses. Those who wish to teach the course over a 12- or 13-week period may simply follow the lesson arrangement as it is given in this *Guide,* using or excluding review/examination sessions as desired.

For 10 sessions, the class may combine four of the shorter lessons into two. The same procedure should be followed for five sessions. However, if the material is to be covered in five sessions, each one should be two hours long with a 10-minute break near the middle. Divide the text chapters among the sessions as needed.

An Alternate Approach
The lesson plans outlined for each session in this *Guide* assume that class members are reading their texts before each class meets. The teacher should make every effort to spark interest in the text by giving members provocative assignments (as suggested under each session) and by such methods as reading aloud an especially fascinating passage (very brief) from the next week's text.

When for any reason, most of the class members will *not* have read the text in advance, (as when the class meets each evening in Vacation Bible School and members work during the day, or as in the first session, when texts may not have been available previously), a slightly different procedure must be followed.

At the beginning of the period, divide the class into small study groups of from four to six persons. Don't separate couples. It is not necessary for the same individuals to be grouped together each time the class meets—though if members prefer this, by all means allow them to meet together regularly.

As teacher of the class, lead one of the study groups yourself. Appoint a leader for each of the other groups. If people are reluctant to be leaders, explain that they need not teach and that they need no advance knowledge of the subject.

Allow the groups and their leaders as much as half an hour to study the textbook together. Then reassemble the class. Ask leaders to report findings or questions of unusual interest or that provoked disagreement. Ask the class the questions you want discussed, and allow questions from your students. Be sure to summarize in closing, what has been studied. Finally, urge each member of the class to make some specific application of the lesson to his life. Use any of the material in this *Guide* that is appropriate and for which you have time.

For additional help, see Kenneth Gangel's *24 Ways to Improve Your Teaching* (Victor, 1974).

Instructions for Victor Multiuse Transparency Masters

The removable center section in this guide provides Victor Multiuse Transparency Masters as important helps for your teaching of this course. They are numbered consecutively and show with what sessions they should be used. The guide gives specific directions for when and how to use each MTM in the lesson material.

To remove the MTMs, open up the two staples in the center of this book and pull out the MTMs. Close the staples again to keep the rest of your guide together. Straighten out the MTMs and file them flat in a regular file folder.

Making Transparencies

You may make your own transparencies inexpensively through the use of these transparency masters. This can be done in at least three ways:

1. Thermal copier (an infrared heat transfer process such as 3M's Thermofax is probably the fastest). Simply pass the MTM with the appropriate film on top of it through the copying machine (at the correct setting). The color portions printed on the MTM are designed not to reproduce.

2. Electrostatic process (such as Xerox). Take care to use the correct film for the right machine. Make sure the glass is clean. Some color on the MTM will come out gray. On certain MTMs some information, printed in a special light color, will NOT reproduce on machine-made transparencies. This gives you extra information to share orally or to write onto the transparency. This way you can control attention by adding material step-by-step. (You'll have all the "answers" on the original MTM.)

3. Trace your own MTM on a transparency film. With minimum artistic ability, you can place a sheet of film over the MTM and trace the major parts of the illustration. Exactness is not necessary and stick figures can be drawn over the printed figures. Block letters can be traced over the printing on the MTM. For best results, use clear 8½″ x 11″ sheets of polyester or mylar film (acetate works, but curls).

To write on the transparencies, use fiber-tip pens. You should have "erasable" or nonpermanent pens if you wish to reuse the film (these wash off with a damp cloth). Use permanent pens if you want to reuse the same visual aid. You may want to make the basic image with a permanent pen and add other material as needed with an erasable pen.

By tracing your own transparencies, you can make overlays. To do this, trace different parts of the *same* MTM onto *different* sheets of film. First, show only one part of the illustration on the bottom film. As the lesson progresses, lay other films on top of it to complete the MTM.

Don't give up if you don't have access to a copying machine. Try your public library, a school, or a printer. Or maybe there's a machine at your office, or at a friend's. Usually arrangements can be made, either by paying for the film or by bringing your own.

Other Uses of Transparency Masters
   1. Spirit masters or mimeo stencils. From these masters or stencils you can run off material for each group member. Both of these can be made on a 3M Thermofax copier. From the master or stencil, as many copies as needed are then made on any spirit duplicator (such as a "ditto" machine) or mimeograph. The MTM may also be traced by hand or typed onto a spirit master or mimeograph stencil.
   2. Visuals. For small groups, the MTMs may be used just as they are, as printed visual aids. It would be helpful to tape them to pieces of cardboard and then prop them up. Or you could put MTMs inside clear "report covers" and write on them.
   3. Chalkboards. You may want to use the MTMs just as you do the other visual sketches in the guide. Copy the MTM illustration onto a chalkboard, flip chart, poster board, or sheet of newsprint, and use it as needed in your presentation.

Recommended Materials
   1. Fiber-tip transparency pens for writing on film:
   "Erasable" (removable with water from any film), such as Sanford's "Vis-a-Vis."
   "Permanent" (removable with rubbing alcohol from acetate, mylar, or polyester), such as Sanford's "Sharpie" (Sanford Ink Co., 2740 Washington Blvd., Bellwood, IL 60104; 312/547-6650).
   2. Clear or colored polyester (or mylar) film sheets for tracing or writing (Transilwrap Corp., 2615 N. Paulina, Chicago, IL 60614; 312/528-8000).
   3. Thermal process film (also called infrared) for machines such as the 3M Thermofax. Transparency film in many colors, as well as spirit duplicator or mimeograph stencils, can all be "imaged" in four seconds on a Thermofax (3M Business Products, 303 Commerce Dr., Oak Brook, IL 60521; 312/920-4271).
   4. Film for electrostatic copiers, such as Xerox (Arkwright-Interlaken Co., Main St., Fiskeville, RI 02823; 401/821-1000).
   NOTE: These companies are manufacturing sources, but each can sell to you directly or refer you to dealers in your area. One convenient retail outlet for ALL of these items is Faith Venture Visuals, Inc., 510 East Main St., Lititz, PA 17543; 717/626-8503.
   5. Two excellent resource books:
   How to Make and Use Overhead Transparencies by Anna Sue Darkes (Moody, 1977).
   Use Your Overhead by Lee Green (Victor, 1979).

The Hidden Child in Us All / *Text, Introduction, Chapter 1*

SESSION GOALS
1. To understand the basic thesis of Dr. Seamands' book.
2. To recall some of the thoughts, experiences and moods of our childhood years.
3. To observe the importance and impact of the "hidden child" in our daily lives as adults.

PREPARATION
1. In the introduction and opening chapter, Dr. Seamands sets forth the basic premise on which he builds throughout the remaining chapters. Before this first session, read through the entire book so that you have a sense of direction about where the course is going. This will enable you to guide discussion away from topics that are dealt with in later chapters.
2. If possible, it will be helpful to spend some time studying Dr. Seamands' first book, *Healing for Damaged Emotions* (Victor). Recommended especially are chapters 1, 4, and 12 which will give the teacher some added background regarding the wounds of childhood.
3. Make sure that the setting for your study is conducive to open, non-threatening communication. Seating arrangements can make a difference. If you wish to encourage discussion, be sure that participants are seated in as small a circle as possible. Make certain that all class members have a copy of the text. Encourage them to bring a pen and notebook to each class as well. Suggest that class members keep a journal of their personal thoughts as they read through the text. The journals can be read at various intervals in the course as introduction to a particular discussion, or as springboards for prayer time at the conclusion of class.
4. Make sure that you have MTM-1 and VS-1 prepared prior to class time. In addition, you need paper, two or three sheets of newsprint, and a magic marker.
5. Pray that God will give insight and discernment. This book deals with issues about which there is much confusion and disillusionment. Ask the Holy Spirit to be the teacher and comforter.
NOTE: It is a good idea to prepare all of your transparencies now, and be sure that you have an overhead projector for the entire course.

PRESENTATION
1. There is likely to be some stiffness in this first session. With that in mind, it may be helpful to spend a few extra minutes having everyone introduce themselves by giving their name, and with responses to the following: "When I was a child . . . my favorite toy was _____,

my favorite cartoon character was _____, and my hero was _____." If the class members know each other relatively well, you could ask them to write their responses to the three statements without signing their names. Then, see if the group can guess who the respondent is on the basis of the three answers.

2. Introduce the book and the biblical text 1 Corinthians 13:9-11, from which the title comes. Take time to say a few words about the study in terms of the format you will be using, the critical need for an informal atmosphere of sharing and honesty, and any other ground rules you wish to set forth. Explain the importance of each person keeping current in the reading, and keeping a weekly journal in reaction to the reading.

3. Moving toward openness, ask each person to respond to this question: **What TV show would best characterize your family during your years of childhood: "Leave it to Beaver," "The Waltons," "The Andy Griffith Show," "The Brady Bunch," "All in the Family," "Dallas"? Why?**

4. Show the class the left portion of MTM-1, "The child is father of the man." Ask the class to respond to this statement in one of four ways: Agree, Strongly Agree, Disagree, Strongly Disagree. Do not feel you must resolve the issue at this time.

5. Leaving MTM-1 in place, read the paragraph which begins, "(The) child that you once were continues to exist within you." Dr. Seamands gives an example of this from his own life. Ask someone to read his account of the episode at the radio station along with his evaluation of it.

Exposing the right side of MTM-1 go on to explain that "the quantity of birthdays may reveal (your) age in life, but the quality of behavior reveals (your) stage in life." Use this quote to say a few words about the negative impact that the hidden inner child can have on our present lives.

6. Now read different versions of the Scripture, 1 Corinthians 13:9-11, and expand on the meaning of the word *katargeo*, which Dr. Seamands defines in detail in the Introduction.

Ask: • **How would you compare Paul's admonition in 1 Corinthians 13:9-11 with what Jesus says in Matthew 18:2-5? Can we make a distinction between childlikeness and childishness?** • **What is the difference?** • **What are some elements of childlikeness that might, in fact, make us**

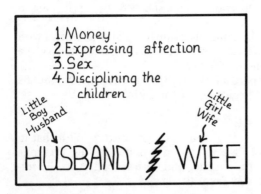

VS-1
The hidden child of the past makes itself known in the home, especially in times of conflict.

better adjusted as adults?

7. Make it clear that this is not "Psych. 101" and that your point here is not to dig far enough and deep enough into the past so that people can find someone to blame their problems on.

• **To what degree can the children be free from blame because of their father's influence?** Dr. Seamands writes that it is "self-defeating irresponsibility" for people to say, " 'My mother and dad, my brother, my circumstances, my teacher, or that accident made me what I am today.' "

• **What point do you think he is making?** • **How does this compare to what Moses said (Exodus 34:7) about the "sins of the fathers" being visited upon the children to the third and fourth generation?**

8. "The little child of the past makes itself most clearly known in the place where a child is most comfortable — in the home and in close personal contacts and in relationships which feel most like home." In the marriage relationship conflicts can surface because "that hidden child of the husband or of the wife wants to run the home." There are four areas where the battle is usually fought. Show these four areas to the group using VS-1 and ask the class to share which problem they feel is most responsible for marital troubles in our culture today. To further clarify how these clashes take place, have a class member read one or both of the examples Dr. Seamands gives — the husband who becomes "the frightened little boy again with Mom fussing at me," or the wife who is haunted by memories of her father everytime her husband spanks the children.

9. Close this session by reading 1 Corinthians 13:1-7, reminding the group that this is the context in which the Apostle Paul is saying to "put away childish things." The tragedy of our holding on to that inner child, and being held by him, is that we cannot be free to enjoy and give the sort of creative love Paul is talking about here.

10. Give the class a "Love Test." List the qualities of creative love on a sheet of newsprint as the class draws them from 1 Corinthians 13. Then, have members rate themselves on a scale of: Poor — Needs work — OK — Making progress — Creatively loving. And as they evaluate themselves, you can suggest that perhaps in those areas where they scored poorly and need work, they are being haunted by a hidden child of the past.

Remind the group that the Holy Spirit can begin to work in these areas of our lives to enable us to *katargeo* the childish things. You may close with a moment of silent prayer as each person reviews his test evaluation and his needs with the Holy Spirit.

ASSIGNMENT

1. Read chapter 2 of the text and write a response in your journal.
2. Recall one positive and one negative memory from your childhood.

The Healing of the Memories / *Text, Chapter 2*

SESSION GOALS
1. To understand the awesome power of the past locked in the memories.
2. To appreciate the need for the healing of the memories.
3. To set forth a practical process to apply the suggestions of this chapter.

PREPARATION
1. Read chapter 2 very carefully. It deals with some very profound and vital spiritual dynamics. Also, read chapters 1 and 2 of *Healing for Damaged Emotions.*
2. In Dr. Seamands' book, *Healing for Damaged Emotions,* he observes that there are two major causes of emotional problems among most evangelicals: "the failure to understand, receive and live out God's unconditional grace and forgiveness; and the failure to give out that unconditional love, forgiveness and grace to other people" (p. 29). It may be apparent to you that one of these dimensions of failure is particularly common in your personal, group, or congregational situation. Keep this in mind as you walk through this lesson with your group and be sensitive to what might be going on inside some of your class members as you deal with these matters.
3. Prepare MTM-2, VS-2 and VS-3. Bring newsprint and magic markers.

PRESENTATION
1. Begin this session with some comments about the mind. Scientists tell us that the average brain weighs about three pounds and consists of roughly three trillion brain cell connections. Dr. Gehard Dirks, one of the chief developers of the IBM computer, commented, "If we could invent a computer that would duplicate the capabilities of the human brain, it would take a structure the size of the Empire State Building, just to house it" (*The Battle for the Mind,* Tim LaHaye, Revell, p. 13). Of the remarkable qualities of brain, one of the most important for us to consider in relation to this session is the subconscious or preconscious mind. Ask class members to give a quick response to the question, **What do you think of when you hear the phrase "subconscious or preconscious mind"?** Briefly share Dr. Seamands' understanding of these terms. You may want someone to read aloud of the discovery of insulin by Dr. Frederick G. Banting.
2. Using MTM-2, build on the discussion by showing the impact of negative memories from childhood on our present lives as adults. Introduce the phrase "healing of the memories" by asking the group to share their answers to this question: • **What does Dr. Seamands mean when he uses the**

phrase, "the healing of the memories"?

Have the class recall the story of Mike. Using a sheet of newsprint, write down everything positive the group suggests about Mike. Underline the fact that Mike was a deeply committed Christian, and that his struggles were not the result of unconfessed sin. Have someone graphically recount that very ugly memory Mike had of his father's shutting him up in the barn for disciplinary purposes. Then, have another person in the group share the remainder of the episode recalling the time of prayer and healing shared by Mike and Dr. Seamands.

• **When was the turning point for Mike?** There may be some varying answers to this question. Have people explain why they consider a certain point the turning point. Depending on class discussion, and how well you feel the group has perceived the importance of the healing of the memories, you may want to follow a similar procedure in looking at the case of Anne.

3. Turn now to VS-2 and give a quick word of explanation about the four kinds of inner children that most commonly haunt people. Have the group choose which of these "hurting children" best characterize Mike and/or Anne. Remember that "sometimes it is a terrible mixture of all four" (*Text*).

• **Given our modern culture, which types of hurting children are we most apt to be raising?**

VS-2
The inner children of the past usually fall into these four categories.

The hurt child   The hating child

The horrified child   The humiliated child

VS-3
Jesus led Peter to restoration in a setting similar to the one in which he denied the Lord.

Similarities

In the courtyard:	On the beach:
· charcoal fire	· charcoal fire
· Peter present	· Peter present
· Jesus present	· Jesus present
· Peter questioned three times	· Peter questioned three times

John 18:15-18,25-27 ➜ John 21:8-9,12,15-17

11

4. Divide your class into six groups. Point out the six suggestions regarding the healing of the memories. Assign one suggestion to each group. Have them read the paragraph and then reduce it to a phrase that they will write on a sheet of newsprint. After a few minutes, have each group explain its suggestion.

5. The Holy Spirit may be speaking to some in your group about one or more of these areas of pain mentioned in this lesson, or He may be convicting some of their need to confess their bondage to some hidden child. Resist the temptation to allow the group to play "amateur psychiatrist." On the other hand, be prepared for the sort of ministry that James speaks of (5:16). Instruct the group to separate from one another so that they create a little space for themselves to think about these questions: • **What is your most positive childhood memory?** • **Your most painful childhood memory?**

6. Still in this mood of reflection and quietness, refer them again to the four "hurting children." • **Is one of these "hurting children" causing pain in your life?** • **Which of the six suggestions would you be willing to follow in the next week to initiate some healing in this area?**

7. Using VS-3, discuss the circumstances surrounding Peter's encounter with Jesus on the beach near the burning coals. Highlight the significance of both encounters—the moment of betrayal and the moment of restoration—taking place in a similar setting. Remind the group of what Peter's thoughts and feelings might well have been on both occasions.

Before closing the session with prayer, ask, • **What beach, which charcoal fire, which memory does Jesus need to take you back to, so that He can bring you healing for those painful memories?** As you pray, be aware that God may be taking some back to that place of pain, so that like Mike and Anne, and even Peter, they can restore that relationship with God and others.

ASSIGNMENT
1. Read chapter 3 of the text and make some response in your journal.
2. Make a list of the mottoes you heard or lived by as a child.

Childhood Mottoes Which Destroy Adults / Text, Chapter 3

SESSION GOALS
1. To understand the impact of childish concepts of God and the Christian life.
2. To discover a process whereby these destructive childhood concepts can be put away and replaced by more biblical ones.

PREPARATION

1. In chapter 3, Dr. Seamands begins to deal with some of the childish things that need to be put away if we are to grow as men and women of God. He deals with wrong concepts of God and the Christian life which quite often are born out of well-meant, but inaccurate and unhelpful childhood mottoes. Ask God to give you insight into some of the "mottoes" that prevail in your group. Perhaps, by now, you have picked up some clues about the sort of childhood mottoes that are a part of their world.

2. Read chapters 7, 8, and 9 in Dr. Seamands' book, *Healing for Damaged Emotions.* Chapter 7, in particular, has some very important comments in regard to the way Christians often derive their appraisals of God's acceptance of them from what their consciences tell them, rather than from what God tells them.

3. Prepare VS-4 on newsprint with only the right side of the visual complete. This will allow you to invite the students to fill in the left side drawing from their own reading.

4. Write out a short definition of the words "complex" and "emotional mechanisms" as Dr. Seamands uses them. These may be written on a sheet of newsprint and put up in the room.

PRESENTATION

1. Ask the group to recall the childhood mottoes they were most influenced by. After several have had a chance to respond to this question, raise the issue of just how much those mottoes become a part of our thinking as adults. Particularly in the realm of our thinking about God and our relationship to Him, many people are more influenced by mottoes of childhood than the message of the Gospel.

If further explanation is needed, have someone read about the young pastor named Brad. Highlight that it is this childish picture of God, never pleased, always demanding, that so many of us carry over from our childhood years. Certainly, this "God" would be impatient with our shortcomings, unsympathetic to our struggles, and harsh in our failures—a "God" who "ups the ante" everytime we feel we can almost be a part of the action.

2. Explain that this sort of immature thinking about God can have serious consequences about the way we handle our relationships. Take time here to define the term "complex" as an "unhealthy emotional push from the past" (*Text*). These complexes force us to use various emotional mechanisms to meet our needs. Use your newsprint definition as you explain.

Draw the important connection between these complexes and emotional mechanisms, and our everyday Christian experience. To present VS-4, comment on how Tournier has likened the Christian life to a revolution (see *Text*). Showing the right side of VS-4, have the group fill in the left side.

3. Dr. Seamands points out, "Christian experience does not of itself automatically cure these complexes or reprogram unhealthy childhood mottoes." On the other hand, we recognize Christ as the new ruler and come to a point of surrender, but there are several pockets of resistance and

strongholds which still need to be uncovered and dealt with. Some of these are the result of these unhealthy inner pushes from the past. Referring to MTM-3, show the tension caused in our lives by two of the most common emotional mechanisms, inferiority and impeccability. Take a moment to ask the class how each complex is defined by Dr. Seamands.

4. Then raise this question: • **Where do you see yourself in these Siamese twins?** Begin a discussion of the impeccability complex by asking, • **When does the healthy pursuit of excellence become an unhealthy striving after standards which are beyond our reach?** • **How do we keep a healthy balance here?** Have the group read Philippians 2:12-13. Paul gives us a balance between our responsibility to work out our own salvation and the fact that God is at work in us. • **How does this verse come into play here?**

• **What solutions to this dilemma can we find in Hebrews 5:12 – 6:1?** Be sure that you explain that the process of sorting out the healthy pursuit from the unhealthy striving is not eliminated with a quicky cliche. Rather, it is this process of learning to differentiate which is "an essential part of leaving spiritual babyhood and growing up into spiritual adulthood" (*Text*). It will take time. It may take the help of a trusted friend or a pastor or a Christian counselor.

5. Moving to the inferiority complex that plagues many Christians, ask, • **When does Christian humility, a recognition that I am not all I can be in Christ, become self-depreciation that is unhealthy?** • **How are we to understand Paul's comments in the following verses?** 1 Corinthians 15:9; 1 Timothy 1:15; 1 Corinthians 4:16; 11:1. • **Do you agree with this statement — Self-depreciation can be as egotistically satisfying and self-centered as self-inflation and pride?**

An inferiority complex can affect our relationships with God and others, as well as with ourselves. In his book, *You're Someone Special* (Zondervan 1978), Bruce Narramore speaks of a study of over 100 Christian high school students which dramatically demonstrated the connection between love for ourselves and perception of God's love. Students who had the highest level of self-esteem (opposite of inferiority complex) viewed God as loving and kind, while students who had an inferior view of themselves tended to see God as stern, angry, vindictive, and impersonal. If our ideas about God are

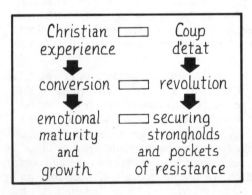

VS-4
Use to explain Paul Tournier's comparison of the Christian life to a revolution.

14

based on incorrect childhood concepts, they can affect the ideas we have about ourselves.

6. Dr. Seamands gives two suggestions for dealing with these unhealthy emotional pushes from childhood. Recount these and ask, • **What are some ways we can distinguish between the voice of God, the voice of conscience, and what is actually the voice of an incorrect childhood motto being replayed in our minds?** • **How did Peter exhibit the "all-or-nothing-at-all" syndrome that is often manifest by these roller coaster mood swings?** See Matthew 17:1-4; John 13:5-9, 36-38; 18:25-27.

7. Have someone in the group read Romans 8:1-2, 31-34 aloud. Then ask the group members to write out a one sentence paraphrase of Paul's ideas here. Paul twice uses the word "condemn." In the first instance he writes, there is "now no condemnation for those who are in Christ Jesus." In the second case he writes, "It is God who justifies; who is to condemn?" Despite all of our childhood "measure up-type" mottoes, in Christ there is no condemnation.

8. Our complexes drive us generally in one of two directions. We either *condemn* ourselves as inferior and unworthy of God's acceptance, or we *compare* ourselves to some impossible standard and judge ourselves unworthy of God's approval.

With all class members in an attitude of prayer, ask the following questions: • **Do you love yourself less than God does?** • **Do you accept yourself less than God does?** • **Do you forgive yourself less than God does?** • **Is there some motto or concept coming back from childhood to haunt you and condemn you?** • **Will you ask the Holy Spirit to help you *katargeo* it, to put it away from your life?**

9. With heads still bowed, close this session by reading a prayer by Dr. A. W. Tozer with which Dr. Seamands concludes chapter 3.

ASSIGNMENT

1. Next week, we will be talking about emotions. In preparation for that discussion, we will participate this week in an "emotional scavenger hunt." Without using any artificial situations (TV, movies, etc.), make a note of each different type of emotion you observe in the coming week and jot down a word or two so that you can recall the context. The emotion may be one you observe in yourself or in others. The following is a list of emotions and feelings that one might see: anger, disappointment, affection, concern for others, cowardice, fear, confidence, cockiness, suspicion, pride, happiness, depression, guilt, dejection (left out), inferiority, embarrassment, frustration, shyness, feeling offended or intimidated, etc.

NOTE: It may be helpful to copy this list for group members and pass it out with the above assignment. Tell members to add to the list if possible.

2. Read chapter 4 of the text and make some kind of response in your journal.

Another Childhood Motto / *Text, Chapter 4*

SESSION GOALS
1. To see how childish ideas affect adult behaviors.
2. To learn the legitimacy of emotions we generally consider non-Christian.
3. To learn to live with our feelings instead of denying them.

PREPARATION
1. In this chapter, Dr. Seamands continues his study of how ideas left over from childhood can have a profound effect on the way we live as adults. In particular, he deals with the fallacy that "Good Christians don't express their true feelings" or, stated another way, "Good Christians must never express any negative feelings."
2. Prepare MTM-4 and VS-5. Have MTMs 1 and 3 handy for review.
3. Try to get a copy of *The Velveteen Rabbit,* by Margery Williams (Doubleday & Co., Inc.). One suggested way of closing this session will be to read pages 16 to 24 of this children's book, to demonstrate the difference between a "toy Christianity," based on childhood mottoes, and a real Christianity appropriate for adult believers. The section to read begins with, "The Skin Horse had lived longer in the nursery than any of the others. . . ." and concludes with, "He was Real. The Boy himself had said it."

PRESENTATION
1. Begin this session by reading this article from the monthly newsletter, *Sources and Resources* (Sampler Edition).
   "How do 'old sayings' reflect young thinking? An elementary school in Baltimore decided to find out. They gave third through fifth grade students the first part of several adages and asked the children to complete them. This is what they came up with:
   'Don't put all your eggs in . . . your pocket.'
   'Don't bite the hand that . . . has your allowance in it.'
   'All is fair in love and . . . fighting with your brother.'
   'If at first you don't succeed . . . blame it on your teacher.'
   'Children should be seen and . . . given triple scoops of ice cream every hour!'"
   Childhood mottoes sometimes have very destructive influences on adult patterns of thinking, even when they aren't garbled. Review the point that "(The) child that you once were continues to exist within you. That hidden child of your past is alive and continues to affect everything you do, for good or for ill" (*Text,* chapter 1). Display MTM-1 while you review this.

Then, while displaying MTM-3, review last week's thought that many people are influenced by childhood concepts that are based on unhelpful mottoes, i.e., "Measure up" or "God helps those who help themselves." Often these lead into two different complexes, inferiority and impeccability.

2. Use this time as a springboard into still another harmful childhood motto: "Brave boys don't cry." While displaying MTM-4, have someone in the group read this portion of the text: "Some of us have had this deadly childhood motto so woven into our lives that as adults we are simply not able to express our real feelings. If feelings do surface, we don't know how to handle them, let alone express them. We feel ashamed or afraid or dirty or weak" (*Text*).

3. Have the group get out their "emotional scavenger hunt" and list on the board or on newsprint the various emotions that people observed. Go back through the list and have the group vote on each emotion from the standpoint of its appropriateness for a strong Christian. Tell them to rate the emotion low if they feel that a person is acting unchristian if he exhibits or feels this emotion; to rate it high if they do not feel that way. After the voting, note which feelings are more or less taboo. Say, "We think we are poor Christians for even having the emotions whether we express them or not. The translation of "Brave boys don't cry" is, "Good Christians don't express their true feelings," or "Good Christians must never express any negative feelings." • **Why do we feel this way?**

4. We have accepted some harmful fallacies as fact. One of them is that to be "a really victorious Christian means we should always be quiet, calm, and unruffled. We should never be grieved or upset, sorrowful or angry — or moved much by anything." • **What verses might lead someone to accept this errant concept of the Christian life?** See Isaiah 26:3; Philippians 4:4-6; 1 Thessalonians 5:16-18. List these and others on the board.

5. Caught in this dilemma, people find themselves trapped in a vicious cycle. Use VS-5 to explain this cycle. There are three major areas in which this cycle can draw us into its spiral.

• Grief and sorrow. • **What are some ways we attempt to deal with our emotions when we are grieved or sorrowful?** It may be helpful to list some of these in a column on a sheet of newsprint or on the board.

VS-5
We can get caught in a vicious cycle
of failure, emotionally.

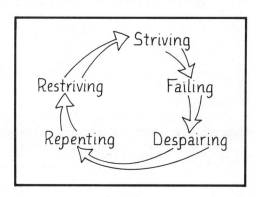

Calling the group's attention to Matthew 14:12-23 and John 11:33-42, ask, • **How did Jesus deal with grief and sorrow?** Dr. Seamands notes that Jesus withdrew from the crowd on the occasion of his hearing about John's death. • **When does withdrawal cease to be healthy and begin to be harmful?** Highlight the difference between grieving over someone you have lost, and grieving for yourself.
   • Anger. Read Mark 3:1-5. • **Does His anger make Jesus any less a perfect Saviour for us?** • **Why or why not?** • **Why wasn't Jesus' anger sinful?** Paul said that we can be angry and yet not sin. See Ephesians 4:26. • **At what point does anger become sin?** Dr. Seamands writes that "Anger is not necessarily the opposite of love. Sometimes it is the result of love and its clearest expression" (*Text*). Ask your group to give examples of this. This chapter counsels us to pray not that our anger will be eradicated, but that it be redirected. • **What is the difference?**
   • A troubled spirit. Look at Jesus' time of prayer in Gethsemane, Mark 14:38-48. • **How would you characterize His "troubled spirit"?** • **Why doesn't Jesus' struggle in this passage demonstrate a lack of victory or a lack of faith?** • **How does one balance being honest about a troubled spirit with verses like Philippians 4:4-6?** • **What about the person who seems to always be down or depressed?** • **When does a troubled spirit genuinely become a signal of spiritual weakness?**
   6. Dr. Seamands writes, "Any experience for which you do not make the required payment of emotion, you will later pay for with compound interest" (*Text*). • **Just what does this principle mean in our lives?** Don't hurry over this question.
   7. In this chapter, Dr. Seamands makes a number of statements that are contrary to popular opinion even among Christians:
   • "There are no sinful emotions. There are sinful uses of any and every emotion . . ." • "Anger is not weakness, rather it is great strength. The Bible nowhere condemns anger as a feeling." • "Mature holiness is recovering our true humanness." Perhaps the group will have others to add. • **Which of these statements do you consider the most significant? Why?**
   8. If you were able to obtain *The Velveteen Rabbit,* invite the group to close their eyes and listen as you read. When you have finished, ask members, in an attitude of prayer to consider, • **How real is your Christian life?** • **Is it just a pretty toy, nothing but a childish plaything based on childish mottoes?** • **Or is it a real, adult Christianity?**
   9. Invite the group members to pray together, specifically thanking Jesus for His perfect humanity and that He understands what it is like to be _____ (grieved, sorrowful, angry, confused, troubled in spirit), whatever is most encouraging to them.

ASSIGNMENT
   1. Ask three different people to give you a definition of love. Record their answers. Write out your own definition as well.
   2. Read chapter 5 of the text. Jot down your weekly entry in your journal.

Childish Ideas of Love and Marriage / *Text, Chapter 5*

SESSION GOALS
1. To reflect on various childhood notions of love and marriage and how they affect adult marriages.
2. To understand the three biblical words for love and what part each is to play in Christian marriage.
3. To get some practical insights on communication within marriage.

PREPARATION
1. Dr. Seamands spends most of this chapter talking about the marriage relationship. Your group may not be composed totally of married couples. As you prepare for this lesson, consider the needs and life situations of your class, and be prepared to aim questions targeted for them. Consider the ways that the material may also be applied to our peer relationships in general.
2. Dr. Seamands begins this chapter by reviewing the recent statistical evidence of the crises in American marriages today. Remember that you may well have some victims of this turmoil in your group. Be sensitive as you choose your words. Pray for an honest, discerning spirit as you teach.
3. If possible, as people arrive, have some music playing with romantic themes. This may serve as a springboard for discussion about ideas of love.

PRESENTATION
1. Begin this session by playing several different "love songs" ranging from the '50s to movie soundtracks to standards like "Let Me Call You Sweetheart." After each song ask group members to tell how it seems to define love. Playing the soundtrack from a movie like "On Golden Pond" has the added advantage that it includes some dialogue.

Dr. Seamands implies that most of our modern definitions of love are not accurate in a biblical sense. Ask members to report some of the definitions of love that they collected. After several have shared, have the class vote on the definitions of love.

After they have arrived at their favorite definitions ask: • **What is wrong with our modern concept of love in this culture?**

Our culture seems to understand love as "a mysterious force from outer space that unexpectedly (seizes) two people, overpowering them, that it is beyond rational control" (*Text*). • **Is this apparent from the songs the group heard or from the definitions given to group members?**

2. Dr. Seamands begins this chapter with statistics on the break-up of marriages. After citing some of those statistics, ask, • **What was wrong with these marriages?** • **Why did they come apart?** • **Were these people not "in love"?**

3. Dr. Seamands sees childish ideas of love and marriage as a major reason marriages come apart. He uses the term "romantic infantilism." Ask someone in the group to define this. • **What is the difference between REEL love and REAL love?**

4. Syndicated columnist Sydney Harris did a very good piece which illustrates the problems that arise when REEL love does not mature into REAL love:

He married her because, among other things, her hair looked so beautiful. . . .

He divorced her because she spent so much time fixing her hair.

She married him because his muscles rippled when he swam. . . .

She divorced him because he spent more time in the bedroom doing sitting-up exercises than anything else.

He married her because she was such an adept conversationalist, never at a loss for words. . . .

He divorced her because she never got off the telephone.

She married him because he could support her in lavish style. . . .

She divorced him because he had too firm a hold on the purse strings.

He married her because all the other men were so impressed with her magnificent figure. . . .

He divorced her after the third child because "she had let herself go."

She married him because he was so courteous and attentive in all the little things that matter so to a woman. . . .

She divorced him because he was so punctilious about little things and so oblivious to important things.

(*Strictly Personal,* Field Enterprises, Inc. 1966)

5. Dr. Seamands mentions a TV show in which a couple vowed to love each other "so long as we both shall *love*." In changing just one letter, the couple "espoused a totally different philosophy of marriage than that which promises to love 'as long as we both shall live' " (*Text*). • **Why is this so?**

6. Divide into groups of three. Give each group a sheet of newsprint and a marker, and a word to define—eros, philia, or agape.

After they write their definitions, take some time to discuss each type of love. • **Which love is most often expressed in our culture?** • **Which love is most important for a good marriage?** • **Is any type of love unimportant in a good marriage?**

7. Most marriages lack good communication. This might be the right place for a role play between a husband and a wife. In the first instance, demonstrate poor communication, by not listening to each other, speaking in cliches, not being really honest, using sarcasm to hurt one another, etc. In the second instance, demonstrate good communication.

Provide this setting for the role play and then let the actors go: It has been a busy day at the office for Bob and a long day at home for Beth with the three kids. Bob walks in the door and with a quick "hello" and kiss he moves (without breaking stride) into the den to his chair and the paper. Beth has been cooped up all day with the kids and has been looking forward to Bob's homecoming so that she could (a) talk with a human being older than five years old, and (b) share with her husband some real feelings of concern she has been having about her mother lately, concerns that came to a focus today when her mother called to see if Bob, Beth, and the kids could drive down for the weekend (a three-hour trip). Let the actors take both role plays from the point of Bob's long-awaited arrival home.

Dr. Seamands writes that "a husband and wife are always communicating with one another, in one way or another" (*Text*). • **What were some of the messages being communicated in various ways in these role plays?**

8. The key to good marital communication is the same key basic to any genuinely Christian communication, "Speaking the truth in love." Ask someone to read Ephesians 4:15-32. As he reads have people write down anything Paul says relating to Christian speech. For example: verses 25, 26, 29 all relate to Paul's general idea of "speaking the truth in love."

Discuss what it means to "speak the truth in love." • **When, if ever, is it not possible to speak the truth in love?** • **Isn't there some truth which cannot be spoken in love?**

9. Building on this biblical concept of speaking truth in love, take a moment to discuss Dr. Seamands' phrase "constructive conflict," or "fighting like Christians." • **Is there such a thing as "constructive conflict"?** • **What are some marks of unconstructive conflict (childish ways of communicating)?** • **What are some characteristics of "constructive conflict"?**

10. Ask group members to think about the three different kinds of love —eros, philia and agape. • **If you are married, or dating, which of these three types of love is least present in your relationship? Why?**

We may not all be married, but we are involved in relationships in which it is necessary to "speak the truth in love" on a consistent, daily basis. • **Which aspect of this kind of communication is most difficult for you— being *willing to speak*, being willing to speak *the truth*, being able to speak the truth *lovingly*?**

11. In this chapter, Dr. Seamands exposes several fallacies and childish ideas about marriage, love and communication: • "Love is self-sustaining," • "Conflict in marriage is harmful and destructive," • "If we can't say something nice we shouldn't say anything," • "Sticks and stones may break my bones but words can never hurt me," • "I couldn't think of marrying him . . . he's too good a friend of mine," • the concept of "falling in love" itself, • the idea that if a marriage is really spiritual, there need not be *eros* love, • the idea that love is a feeling of being all "shook up." • **Which of these fallacies has been a source of confusion to you?**

12. Lead the group in prayer giving thanks for the growth, enjoyment, and security that comes by hard work in marriage. Use this prayer time to affirm the benefits of marriage and encourage those who may be convicted by some of today's discussion.

ASSIGNMENT

1. Watch the newspapers this week for a specific example of an "innocent" victim who meets tragedy by what appears to be simply a cruel trick of fate—a little child run over by a drunk driver, a terrorist bomb killing a family enjoying a meal together. Bring the article next time.

2. Read chapter 6 of the text and make an entry in your journal.

Childish Ideas of God and His Will
/ *Text, Chapter 6*

SESSION GOALS
1. To understand how many of our attitudes about tragedy and misfortune are reflections of childish ideas about God.
2. To understand how the will of God relates to our disappointments.
3. To understand what is meant by "the will of God."

PREPARATION
1. Read through chapter 6 carefully. Be prepared to discuss this chapter in such a way that people in your group are not threatened by unfamiliar terms and concepts.
2. In a recent issue of *Theology Today,* Ronald Allen, a minister in Grand Island, Nebraska, wrote about his experience of ministry in the wake of a recent series of tornadoes which left almost 1,000 homes in the community destroyed or uninhabitable. His article, "How We Respond to Natural Disaster," provides some helpful insights as you prepare for this lesson. He notes three different types of responses to the natural disaster that had befallen his community:
- "It was just one of those things." This response exhibits a trivial attitude, refusing to take suffering seriously. It approaches tragedy with a half-flippant, half-fatalistic "win some, lose some." Some people consider this the response of faith.
- "The devil was responsible for the storm, and it was because of the faith of Christians that it was no worse than it was." From this perspective, the universe is little more than a giant checkerboard over which hover two players, God and the devil.
- "The judgment of God punishing an evil people."
3. Have chalk or markers ready for VS-6.

PRESENTATION
1. Begin the lesson this week by asking some class members to share the various news accounts of tragedies with innocent victims. After a few accounts, ask members of your class how, in light of their belief in the love, justice, and sovereignty of God, they would explain an event like one of these to the grieving relative of one of the victims.
2. After a few minutes of wrestling with these issues as a class, open up a whole new aspect of the issue by reading the various responses that victims of Grand Island, Nebraska had to their plight. Then, ask three people to read the examples of human tragedy recounted by Dr. Seamands at the outset of the chapter.
- **Based on the comments and questions of these people, how would you**

MTM-2 Use with Session 2 of *Putting Away Childish Things*

STEP 1.
Temptation

STEP 2.
Temptatio
if the will

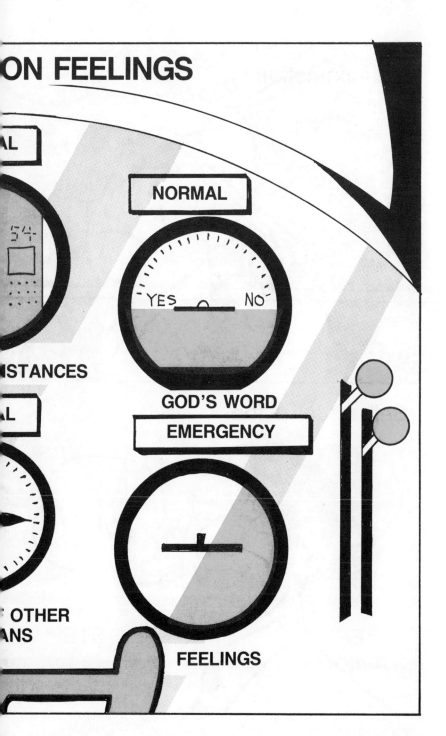

ON FEELINGS

NORMAL

YES — 0 — NO

GOD'S WORD

EMERGENCY

FEELINGS

MTM-8 Use with Sessions 10, 11 of *Putting Away Childish Things*

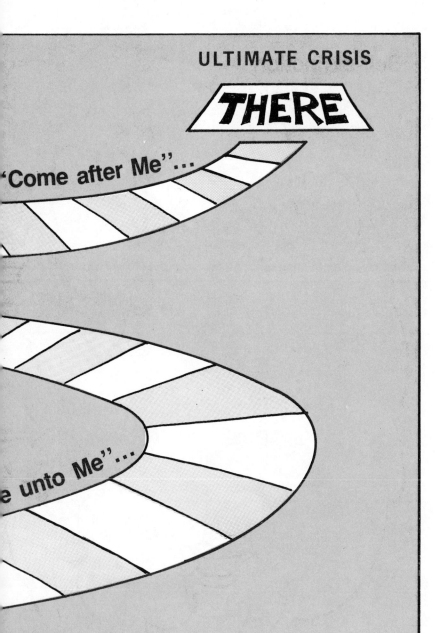

ULTIMATE CRISIS

THERE

"Come after Me"...

e unto Me"...

al Movement
ard God

y.

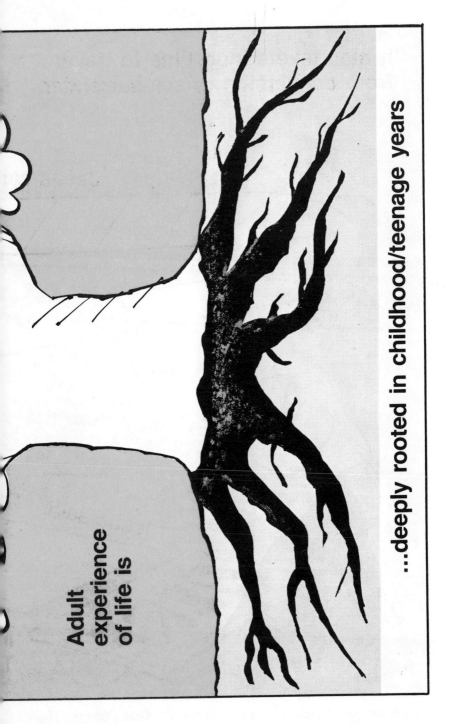

Adult experience of life is

...deeply rooted in childhood/teenage years

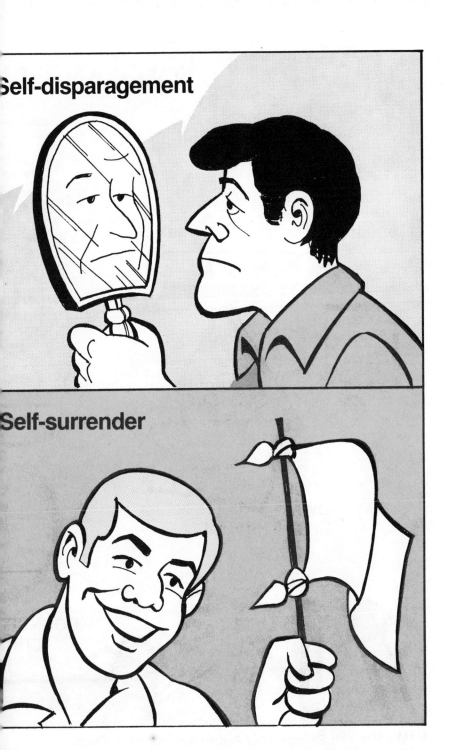

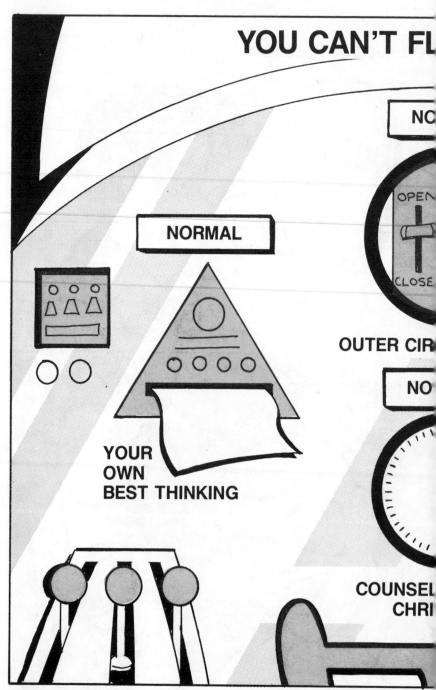

YOU CAN'T FL

NO

OPEN

CLOSE

NORMAL

OUTER CIR

NO

YOUR
OWN
BEST THINKING

COUNSEL
CHRI

MTM-7 Use with Session 9 of *Putting Away Childish Things*

eads to sin
gnored.

STEP 3.
Temptation is checked
by will.

nly.

MTM-5 Use with Session 7 of *Putting Away Childish Things*

MTM-3 Use with Sessions 3, 4 of *Putting Away Childish Things*
©1982 by SP Publications, Inc. Permission granted to purchaser to reproduce this visual for class purp

describe each individual's concept of God? • What concept of God emerges from the person who looks at natural disaster and says, "It's just one of those things"?

• What difference does it make how we understand the will of God? Refer back to Romans 12:1-3, and ask, • How does this passage describe the will of God? • Going back to the man whose home has been leveled by a tornado, or the woman whose child has been taken by some childhood disease, in what sense can these be described as the will of God — good, acceptable and perfect? • Or, if these events occur outside of God's will, then in what sense can God be described as sovereign or all-powerful?

3. The question of how we understand God's will ties in directly with how we understand God. Hence, it is vital that we rid ourselves of childish and unbiblical notions about the phrase "the will of God." Dr. Seamands gives us at least three meanings for this phrase, each of them exemplified in the Scripture and daily life. Ask your group to list these three meanings and give a definition for each. As they give the three meanings, you can record their answers as in VS-6.

4. Looking first at the intentional, perfect will of God, use these questions to stimulate discussion: • How might one be comforted by the idea that his tragedies are the intentional will of God? • How can such a belief lead to resentment? After all, it is a short step from blindly recognizing that "God intended this tragedy to befall me" to "God made this happen to me and if He really cared about me, He would not have let this happen."

• How detailed is the intentional will of God? • Does He care or intend for me to take one route or another to work this week? Dr. Seamands states that "the intentional, perfect will of God can be defeated by the will of man for the time being. If this were not true, humans would have no real freedom whatsoever." This helps to explain how a sovereign God cannot be held responsible for all that happens in the sense that He *intended* it to happen.

5. Now introduce the idea of God's permissive will by reading these words of C. S. Lewis:

In a game of chess you can make certain arbitrary concessions to your opponent, which stand to the ordinary rules of the game as miracles stand to the laws of nature. You can deprive yourself of a castle, or allow the other man sometimes to take back a move made inadvertently. But if you conceded everything that at any moment happened to suit him — if all his moves were revocable and if all your pieces on the board disappeared whenever their positions were not to his liking — then you would not have a game at all. So it is with the life of souls in this world: fixed laws, consequences unfolding by causal necessity, the whole natural order, are at once the limits within which their common life is confined and also the only conditions under which any such life is possible. Try to exclude the possibility of suffering which the order of nature and the existence of free wills involve, and you will find that you have excluded life itself" (*The Problem of Pain,* Macmillan, Ch. 2).

God's intentional, perfect will is at times overruled by the circumstantial, permissive will of God. His perfect will might be that we should always win at checkers, regardless of rules or skills. But this is not checkers. Or life. Therefore, God permits losses, mistakes, and apparent tragedies. This is what Dr. Seamands is talking about when he says, "Many things which are permitted to happen to us in this world are the price of: (1) a world of reliable laws, where we can count on things, and (2) a world of free moral choices" (*Text*).

• **How are we to interpret Romans 8:28 in light of these truths?** You may wish to recall Weatherhead's quote, "Nothing can happen to you that God cannot use for good." • **Does that mean that everything that happens to us is good?** • **Is it possible to make a distinction between giving thanks "in" all things, and giving thanks "for" all things?**

Have two people read Philippians 4:4, 6 and 1 Thessalonians 6:16, 18. Notice the idea of giving thanks *in* all circumstances, rather than giving thanks *for* all things. This recognizes that while everything that happens is obviously not good or something for which we are thankful, we can always in any situation be thankful that God can use the bad circumstance for a good purpose in the lives of the saints.

6. The last area of discussion is the ultimate will of God. Ask someone to read or recall from their reading Weatherhead's illustration of the ultimate will of God. You may further illustrate the ultimate will of God by reading this quote from *The Knowledge of the Holy* (A. W. Tozer, Harper & Row, p. 118):

An ocean liner leaves New York bound for Liverpool. Its destination has been determined by proper authorities. Nothing can change it. This is at least a faint picture of sovereignty. On board the liner are scores of passengers. These are not in chains, neither are their activities determined for them by decree. They are completely free to move about as they will. They eat, sleep, play, lounge on the deck, read, talk, altogether as they please; but all the while the great liner is carrying them steadily onward toward a predetermined port.

The ultimate will of God does not necessarily preclude the possibility of free, responsible human activity. God's omnipotence does *not* mean "that by sheer exhibition of power God gets His own way" (*Text*).

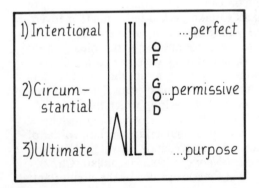

VS-6
Display to illustrate the three levels of the will of God.

7. Read through the following passages and discuss the sense in which the will of God is understood in each passage: 1 Peter 3:17; Ephesians 1:11; 1 Thessalonians 4:3; 2 Peter 3:9; Daniel 4:34-35; Matthew 18:14; Jeremiah 28:11ff.; 2 Chronicles 7:14; Genesis 45:4-8 (explain context). Do not be concerned that all group members agree that a passage speaks of God's will as meaning the same thing.

In closing today, invite group members to take a moment to think about the various episodes in their lives that have involved mishaps, wrong decisions, apparent coincidences. They can think of these and then of other more purposeful decisions as being some part of a small trickle that begins at one point and by God's hand moves eventually to another point. As the class reflects in this moment of quiet, read the following prayer from *Someone Who Beckons* (Timothy Dudley-Smith, IVP):

Lord of my life, how many things have happened to me that might have happened otherwise! Looking back, upon what slender threads Your pattern for me hung! What insignificant weights tilted the scale from this to that! And from this multitude of tiny choices, unrelated circumstances, unnoticed influences, You wove the pattern of my present life! . . . And all this that I recall, only the tip of the iceberg! What of the unseen providences? What of the choices before I was born or thought of? I join, Lord, with the children in their song of praise: "Thank You, Father, for making me me."

And if this is true of my past life, shaped, subtly and beyond imagining, by the finger of God—why, I rest my future on Your promise too. You know Your plans, Lord, as You did for Israel in exile. Knowing that the plans are Yours, I do not need to know much else about them. Except this: that all You do is good. So let me seek You, Lord, Your face, Your Word, Your presence and Your will, with all my heart.   Amen.

Invite class members to make sentence prayers of praise for one aspect of God's will discussed in this section, or one example of God's will demonstrated in their own lives.

ASSIGNMENT

1. Respond in your journal to these two statements: "My greatest discouragement about prayer came when. . . ." "My greatest satisfaction in prayer was when. . . ."

2. Read chapter 7. In the margin of your copy of the book, place a smiling face beside that portion of this chapter which gives you most encouragement; place an exclamation point beside the portion of the chapter that corrects a misunderstanding about prayer that has caused you some confusion.

Childish Ideas of Prayer / Text, Chapter 7

SESSION GOALS
1. To integrate a correct understanding of the will of God with our practices and beliefs about prayer.
2. To identify why some prayers seem to not be answered.

PREPARATION
1. Much of the theological timber the group sawed through last week in the study of the will of God will be used to build a platform for this week's lesson. Be thinking of ways to draw from last week's lesson to bring more into the session this week.
2. Because chapter 7 is slightly longer, it may be helpful to make an outline of the major ideas and the flow of thought as you read through it. It will be better to focus in on a few ideas that you can really clarify, than to cloud the issue by trying to hit too many ideas in one meeting.
3. Childish ideas about prayer cause us to doubt the effectiveness and worthwhileness of prayer. And this being the case, exhortations to pray may fall on deaf ears until the roots of the problem are dealt with. That, essentially, is the point of this chapter. Make it the thrust of your teaching this session. Be willing to share your own frustrations and questions about prayer. This will anchor the lesson in the hearts and lives of your group.
4. Prepare MTM-5. It may be helpful to have VS-6 hung in a place visible to the group, to draw the connection between last week's theological truths and this week's practical application.

PRESENTATION
1. Ask several class members to share their journal responses to the statements about satisfaction and discouragement in prayer.
2. Having introduced the idea of prayer, ask your group to take this survey: **Which of these lines from various TV commercials best characterizes the attitude most people in this part of the country have about prayer? Most people in your church have about prayer? The attitude you have about prayer?**
   • "You asked for it, you got it—Toyota";
   • "Reach out, reach out and touch someone; Call up, call up and just say 'Hi' ";
   • "You, you're the one. We do it all for you";
   • "When E. F. Hutton talks—everyone listens";
   • "Catch that Pepsi spirit, drink it in, drink it in, drink it in";
   • "How do you spell relief?"
Have them explain why they choose the answer they do. They may suggest other commercial slogans.
3. At this point, introduce MTM-5 illustrating one of the major

emphases of this chapter, that half-truths can be deadly, and half-truths in the area of faith and prayer are especially lethal. Quote from Os Guinness' classic book on doubt, *In Two Minds,* (InterVarsity Press), in which he describes the damage and doubts which arise from faulty ideas about God. "The Devil's stock in trade is the world of half-truths and half-lies where the half-lie masquerades as the whole truth." Point out that half-truths about prayer, even those spoken by the most well-intentioned people, can be particularly devastating.

4. Ask someone in the group to read Connie's story from chapter 7. After reading her story, ask, • **What was Connie feeling?** • **Can you think of an instance in your own life when you have felt this way?** • **Was Connie's problem a lack of faith in God?** • **If Connie had come to you for help, how would you have counseled her?** Referring back to MTM-5, observe that Connie is a woman whose faith had been damaged by some half-truths spoken by well-meaning people, and that her prayer life and her attitude toward God were all falling down as a result.

5. We hear that with God all things are possible. • **Is there anything that God can't do?** Dr. Seamands explains that the flip-side to the verse, "With God all things are possible," is the fact that "with God some things are impossible" (*Text*). • **Why is this such a critical point to make?** • **If it is true that God can do all things, isn't it basically the same idea to say that, therefore, God will do all things?**

Ask the class to list those things which, according to Dr. Seamands, God cannot do.

Read each of the following prayers and ask the class to determine which impossibilities of God they ignore.

• "Dear God, I realize I've missed class all week, and I've not read the assigned material, but I pray that You would help me make an A on this exam."

• "Dear God, we need apples more than we need roses—please, help our rose bush to bear apple blossoms and apples this season."

• "Lord, make my son a Christian so that he will turn his life around before it's too late."

• "God, You understand my deep down love for my family. Please try to understand why I have to be deceitful in this business deal."

• "Lord, our daughter is dead and we have no hope left except Your mighty healing power. Please, Lord, bring her back!!"

• Have someone read the example of the missionary in India (*Text*). **Which impossibility of God apparently was ignored in this case?**

• **In the case of Connie—what impossibility of God did her pastor ignore in his counsel to her?**

6. Dr. Seamands writes about the sin of presumption. • **When does faith become presumption?** • **What is the difference between faith, presumption, and expecting a miracle?** • **What about pithy phrases like "Name it and claim it"?** • **Is this presumption?**

Have someone in the group look up the following verses: Proverbs 16:3; Psalm 37:4-6; John 15:7. • **How are we to understand these verses so as to avoid the sin of presumption?** Ask someone in the group to look up

Matthew 26:36-44 and 2 Corinthians 12:8-9. In these two cases, where clearly all conditions for granting a petition were met, those praying did not fall into presumption.

7. This leads you into the final stages of this discussion—the problem of unanswered prayer. Dr. Seamands reviews three reasons that prayers often go "unanswered." Introduce each reason to the group, one at a time.

• The petitioner asks for the wrong things (James 4:3). God distinguishes between our wants and our needs. • **Does that mean that we should ask only for what we really need?** • **How would it affect your prayer life if you knew that you would always get what you prayed for?** • **Would you feel better about praying, or perhaps worse?**

• We ask for things we should be taking care of ourselves. • **What if we could turn all labors over to God by faith through prayer, and God assumed the responsibility—what sort of church would we have?** • **What is the difference between "giving it all to Jesus" and copping out on our responsibilities?** • **Where do we draw the line?**

• We are not ready for God's answer. In this section, we are given two different biblical words for time, *chronos,* the chronological word for time, and *kairos,* which means "the right time and the ripe time." Ask the group to speculate about some reasons why God may not feel the timing is right. Suggested answers might be that someone needs to learn patience, or faith; or that there is still more benefit to be derived from the situation by allowing an individual to suffer; or that a solution at the wrong time might allow someone to draw the wrong conclusions about their own abilities to solve the problem. If further illustration is needed, read the account of St. Augustine's mother.

8. Going back to your journals, ask the group to recall again their most discouraging experience with prayer. Now, however, invite them to view it in light of their observations from this chapter, to explain their struggles in relation to these insights.

9. Ask all group members to take a few moments now and write a letter of thanks to God. Instruct them that these will be read in closing, and that their letters are to begin with the following: "Dear God, I want to thank You that all my prayers aren't answered because . . ."

Draw the session to a close by having some people read their letters as a prayer. Then close in prayer by thanking God that He does sometimes answer our prayers as we wish He would.

ASSIGNMENT

1. List 10 basic distinctions that all of us make in everyday life, e.g., hot—cold, off—on, light—dark, functioning—broken, etc. Bring this list with you to the next session.

2. Read chapter 8 and write in your journal. Especially take time to note which area of confusion and distinction has been most troublesome to you.

3. In chapter 8, Dr. Seamands quotes the adage: "Children are the world's greatest recorders and the world's worst interpreters." Try to recall and record in your journal an example of when your own children—or children you know—have proven this to be true.

Childhood Confusions Versus Adult Distinctions

Text, Chapter 8

SESSION GOAL

To clarify some very basic distinctions vital to a healthy Christian life:

1. The distinction between acceptance and approval: Does approval equal acceptance?

2. The distinction between temptation and sin: Does temptation equal sin?

3. The distinction between hurt and harm: Does God allow me to be harmed if He is allowing me to be hurt?

PREPARATION

1. Study chapter 8.

2. Prepare MTM-6. Have newsprint and markers or a chalkboard available so that they are accessible during the lesson for VS-7.

3. Reproduce copies of VS-8 for members of the class.

PRESENTATION

1. Begin the session today by introducing Dr. Seamands' observation that children are the world's greatest recorders but the world's worst interpreters. Invite members of the group to share episodes from the lives of their own children, or perhaps from their own childhood experiences that substantiate the truth of this old adage. Use this as a springboard for your discussion of how childhood confusions often get carried into adulthood and bring about misinterpretations that are often quite tragic.

2. Ask group members to share some of the daily distinctions with which we live. List these on the newsprint or chalkboard. Emphasize how critical these distinctions are if we are to function effectively from day to day.

3. Move into a discussion of the three important distinctions in this chapter: between acceptance and approval, temptation and sin, and hurt and harm.

Using VS-7 talk about the formula Dr. Seamands mentions in the distinction between acceptance and approval. Be sure that the connection is drawn between parental action and childhood interpretation of that action.

Ask: • **How can we show our children that we disapprove of their actions without leading them to believe that we do not accept them as persons?** • **What about other people, our own peers, who are doing blatant wrong — how do we show disapproval without rejecting them?**

Dr. Seamands writes: " Some of us have never learned that it is possible to hold the highest moral standards and at the same time be accepting and loving toward those who have violated those standards" (*Text*). • **How do** we do this? • When we do not do this, what is it we are so deeply fearful of?

Ask someone to read the biblical accounts of Jesus handling this kind of predicament in John 4:5-42; 8:3-11; Luke 19:1-10. • **Why are we afraid to accept someone whose actions are clearly wrong?** • **How did Jesus show acceptance without diluting the standard of holiness and justice?** Be sure to talk about John 8:11.

• **Why is it so important to make the distinction between acceptance and approval if we want to have a healthy relationship with God?**

4. Moving on to the second important distinction, between temptation and sin, ask someone to read the story of Adam and Eve from Genesis 3:1-13. As group members listen, they should raise their hands at the point where Eve and Adam actually crossed the line of disobedience and sinned. Have the women watch for Eve's point of sin. The men should watch the sin point for Adam. Urge them to be specific, to narrow it down to one phrase, one moment, one motion if possible.

Ask the group to share why they chose the phrase, moment, or motion they did as the point of sin for Eve or Adam. Use this discussion to introduce the difference between temptation and sin. • **When does temptation become sin?** • **Is temptation sin?** Without giving a definite answer, read the ideas by Dante, in chapter 8. • **How does this picture depict the Christian life?** • **What statement does it make about the Christian life?** Underscore the idea that everybody experiences temptation, regardless of age or godliness. You may give examples from Scripture from the lives of men like Joseph (Gen. 39:6-12), David (2 Sam. 11:2-4), Jesus (Luke 4:1-13) — the point being that there is no immunity from temptation.

Have someone read James 1:13-15. • **Where does the temptation come from?** Point out that it does not come from God.

Then, using MTM-6, ask which of the three pictures illustrates sin. Base your thoughts on Dr. Seamands' discussion of the words "lust" and "drawn away" or "enticed" or "lured". In picture 1 of MTM-6 we are still in James 1:14. There is a lure to be sure and there is desire. But, the desire has not been consummated. Therefore, in picture 1, there is no sin. In picture 3 of MTM-6 we move into verse 15. As the desire is fulfilled, we see a picture of sin and death. Picture 2 shows the lure and the desire being separated by a decision of the will so that no sin has taken place. Read James 1:13-15 through again. Now have someone read from the two text paragraphs beginning: "It takes two to conceive in order to give birth to sin."

• **Why is it so vital that we make the distinction between temptation and sin?** • **How can confusion of these damage one's relationship with God?**

5. The final distinction Dr. Seamands highlights is between hurt and harm. Ask someone to read Hebrews 12:5-11. • **How does this passage illustrate the difference between being hurt and being harmed?** Refer also to Jacob (Gen. 32:22-32) and Paul (2 Cor. 12:1-10) to show how God may hurt us in order to help us, but never to harm us. The following poem wonderfully captures the point of this third distinction.

The Shaping of a Disciple
When God wants to drill a man, and thrill a man, and skill a man,
When God wants to mold a man to play for Him the noblest part,

When He yearns with all His heart to build so great and bold a man
That all the world shall be amazed, then watch God's methods, watch
　His ways!
How He ruthlessly perfects whom He royally elects;
How He hammers him and hurts him, and with mighty blows
　converts him,
Making shapes and forms which only God Himself can understand,
Even while His man is crying, lifting a beseeching hand . . .
Yet God bends but never breaks when man's good He undertakes;
When He uses whom He chooses, and with every purpose fuses
Man to act and act to man, as it was when He began;
When God tries His splendor out, man will know what He's about!

Dale Martin Stone

6. As you close together in prayer, challenge group members to consider
which distinction had become most blurred for them, which distinction is
most precious for them. Then in a few moments of group prayer, have them
give thanks to God the Father who accepts us even when He can't approve
our behavior, who never judges us for temptation, only for our sin, and
who will hurt us only so He can heal and help us.

VS-7
Use as you discuss the connection
between acceptance and approval.

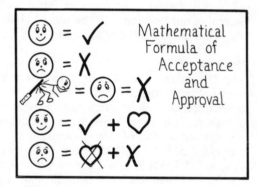

VS-8
From this drawing produce a larger
graph on which members will trace
the emotions of Elijah.

Exuberant	
Bewildered	
Depressed	
Verses	1 Kings 17:1, 4, 7, 9, 12, 15...

ASSIGNMENT

1. Read chapter 9 of the text and make an entry in your journal.

2. On a graph, VS-8, rate the various emotions experienced by the prophet Elijah, in the verses listed here: 1 Kings 17:1, 4, 7, 9, 12, 15, 18, 20, 24; 18:1, 17, 40, 46; 19:3, 4, 5, 19. Bring the graph to the study next week.

3. NOTE TO TEACHER: You will want to locate *My Heart Christ's Home* for Session 11.

Childish Dependency on Feelings / *Text, Chapter 9*

SESSION GOALS

1. To understand how our feelings can be misleading to us, if we depend on them for an accurate reading of our status in relation to God.

2. To understand the role our feelings should and should not play in discerning our obedience to the will of God.

3. To understand the relationship between what we feel and how we act.

PREPARATION

1. The value of this lesson, apart from its specific teaching about our often unhealthy dependency on feelings, is that it begins to bring together some concepts from chapters past. Take some time in beginning this study to draw some of these connections. Guidelines for this will be given in the Presentation section of this session.

2. Have MTM-1, MTM-4, and VS-8 available for this session. Also, bring MTM-7, VS-9, and chalk or markers and newsprint.

3. Be sure that you have spent adequate time preparing your own graph as per the homework assignment. You could put your graph on a clear projection sheet so that everyone can see it during the discussion.

PRESENTATION

1. Using MTM-1, go back again and review the basic premise on which Dr. Seamands' book is based, that childhood misconceptions can lead to destructive patterns in adulthood. This chapter reminds us of two key words of Paul's, in 1 Corinthians 13:11 and 1 Corinthians 3:1. Ask someone to read these two verses, and take a moment to further review the basic premise of the book by sharing the meaning of *katargeo* and *nepios*.

2. Turn now to the graphs, VS-8, and ask two members to share theirs, explaining what action took place and Elijah's reaction. After a few minutes of discussion, observe that even Elijah, the great man of God, still had to deal with and struggle with his feelings. The graphs should demonstrate the

wide range of emotions that Elijah experienced.

3. Becoming a Christian and being solidly committed to God does not guarantee that this struggle with emotions will automatically leave us. "God is not out to alter your fundamental personality structure. . . . One of the healthiest things for a new Christian is to take a good look at himself, accept the basic facts about himself, and not berate himself because he isn't like someone else" (*Text*). • **What factors in our culture make this so hard?**

4. There are three areas of the Christian life which are influenced by our emotions: Feelings and Assurance, Feelings and Guidance, and Feelings and Good Works. List these on the board or on newsprint.

Take three sheets of construction paper and on one sheet write the word Faith, on another Fact, on another Feeling. Ask for three volunteers to come in front of the group and hold the signs. Then, ask class members to give these three volunteers instructions about how they should stand so that they are lined up in order of importance in the Christian life. Ask: • **Isn't faith the most important?** • **What good are the facts if we have no faith in them?** • **Which, if any, of the three is not essential to Christian experience?** While in no way underplaying the value of our emotions and feelings, Dr. Seamands wants to point out that our faith is not dependent on how we feel. Feelings may follow our faith, but we cannot let faith follow feelings.

Divide into three groups, and then have people pair off in each section. Their assignment is to see how David used the facts on which his faith was based to control his feelings, and not vice versa. Assign Psalms 42 and 43, Psalm 63, and Psalm 73. Have each pair examine the feelings David might have been experiencing in their assigned selection, and how he responded to them by referring to the facts of his faith. After about five minutes, have some of the pairs share their answers.

Dr. Seamands gives us this simple formula: "You are not just your feelings. At any given moment you are greater than the sum total of your thoughts and feelings" (*Text*). • **While we might agree that this is true, isn't "living above our feelings" the same as denying our feelings?** • **Why?**

E. Stanley Jones says that sometimes we have to fool ourselves into a new way of acting, but at other times need to act ourselves into a new way of feeling. • **What does this mean?** • **How does this happen in the case of the wife who doesn't feel love for her husband any more?** • **How does this happen for the Christian who doesn't feel "fired up for Jesus" anymore?**

Oswald Chambers has an excellent insight in his book *My Utmost For His Highest* (Dodd, Mead and Co., p. 141) that captures this idea very well:

There are certain things we must not pray about—moods, for instance. Moods never go by praying, moods go by kicking. A mood nearly always has its seat in the physical condition, not in the moral. It is a continual effort not to listen to the moods which arise from a physical condition. Never submit to them for a second. We have to take ourselves by the scruff of the neck and shake ourselves, and we will find that we can do what we said we could not. The curse with most of us is that we won't. The Christian life is one of incarnate spiritual pluck.

5. Ask, • **How do you determine God's guidance in basic decisions you**

make—not just the small decisions, but the big ones? • How important is it to you that a decision you make "kind of feels right"?

Show VS-9 to the group explaining that there are three sources of feelings and impressions. With only the face of the diagram drawn, ask the group to give these three sources. As they are given, draw them into the diagram. • How do you know which of the three is the source of your feelings and impressions? Have someone read 1 John 4:1. • What are some ways we can test the spirits? • Do verses 1-6 of 1 John 4 give any clues? Verses 2 and 6b seem to give some guidance. For other "tests," have group members look up 1 John 3:10 and Deuteronomy 13:1-5.

List on the board or on newsprint five channels of guidance: (1) God's Word, (2) outer circumstances, (3) your own best reasonable thinking, (4) counsel of other Christians, (5) inner voice of feelings. Ask class members to rank these in order of dependability. • Which of these channels of guidance has proven most helpful to you? • Which is most prone to throw someone off the track? • Why? Displaying MTM-7, conclude by retelling the story of the pilot's admonition, "You can't fly by your feelings."

6. We are to do good works even when we don't feel like it. Ask class members to honestly share a recent instance when they did something good despite their feelings. Have a group member read James 4:17 and another read 2 Timothy 4:2. Oswald Chambers comments that the "season" here refers not to times, but to us. He writes:

If we do only what we feel inclined to do some of us would do nothing for ever and ever. There are unemployables in the spiritual domain, spiritual decrepit people, who refuse to do anything unless they are inspired. The proof that we are rightly related to God is that we do our best whether we feel inspired or not (*Ibid*, p. 116).

• If we do good when we do not feel like it, isn't this just hypocrisy? • How does this principle relate to the life of men of God like Moses or Paul? • Or to Jesus, especially in the Garden of Gethsemane?

7. About 10 minutes before the end of the session, ask group members to put away everything but a piece of paper and writing tool. As they rethink today's study, ask them to decide in which of these three areas they most need help. Then remind them of David's psalms—how he saw some areas of

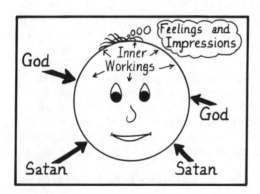

VS-9
It is important to know where our feelings and impressions come from.

need. Rather than dwelling on his negative feelings regarding those areas of need, he focused his eyes on the provision of the Lord. Ask members to take a few moments to compose their own personal psalm of thanksgiving.

After a few minutes, close in prayer by having group members read their psalms aloud.

ASSIGNMENT
1. Read chapter 10 of the text and make a journal entry based on the completion of this sentence; "My own self-image is. . . ."
2. Read Psalm 139 and memorize the one verse most precious to or encouraging for you.

Childish Concepts of Self and Self-Surrender / *Text, Chapter 10*

SESSION GOALS
1. To get a biblical perspective of the self.
2. To evaluate ways to deal with the self.
3. To understand the biblical mandate of self-surrender.

PREPARATION
1. By now, you know your group very well. You should know the kinds of emphases they need. There are four ways of dealing with the self that are mentioned by Dr. Seamands in this chapter. As you read through the lesson before preparing it, keep this question in mind, "Which of these four means of dealing with the self is most apparent in the individuals in our group?" In some churches, the trend from childhood has been to make people feel that the self is an awful, ugly thing and that someone who has any sense of self-love is obviously conceited and ignorant of Scripture. Consequently, many Christians have grown up with the idea that they have had little to offer the church or to their friends. Hymns with phrases like ". . . would He devote that sacred head for *such a worm as I*? . . ." have made the impression that the less we think of ourselves, the more God will be pleased with us. On the other hand, our society overflows with propaganda about how noble is humanity, how the potential of mankind is boundless and how allowing the self to have full expression is the key to real fulfillment.

2. Make sure that you have enough Bibles on hand for everyone, and that you personally have memorized the one verse from Psalm 139 that was most precious, most significant for you.

3. Prepare MTM-8. Also bring newsprint, markers and an old glove.

PRESENTATION

1. Begin this session by writing on the board or on a sheet of newsprint the six terms Dr. Seamands alludes to in the opening paragraph of the chapter. Ask the group to give a definition of each of these terms. • **What do we mean when we talk devotionally about the self?** • **Is the self what we are, or what we do, or what we think?** Some people define themselves in terms of their occupation, their marital status, number of children, etc.

2. Ask someone to read through the paragraph near the beginning of the chapter in which Dr. Seamands relates the circumstances surrounding the death of Dag Hammarskjold. That paragraph concludes with the sentence, "No concept is more important to a mature understanding of what Christ is asking from you" (*Text*). This reading will launch you into the main body of discussion about the four different ways of dealing with the self.

3. **Self-extinction.** Ask for a definition of this idea. • **Is this a biblical idea?** A good visual illustration of the concept involves use of your hand and a glove. Your hand represents your self, and the glove represents your Christian life, your work for the Lord, your identity as a Christian. Many Christians believe that the self is to be totally extinguished, but that belief would leave no muscle or movement in the glove. There would be no means by which God could be served. Someone who prays, "God take the self out of me . . ." is praying something that is not Christian at all. • **What is the difference between the idea of self-extinction and the Christian concept of humility?** • **Is there a difference between Christ saying in John 15:5, "Without Me you can do nothing," and our thinking that we really need to become nothing in order for God to use us?**

4. **Self-disparagement.** Many Christians equate denial of self with self-disparagement because "they do not understand the proper place of self-love in the Christian life" (*Text*). • **What is the proper sense in which we are to love ourselves?** Ask the group to read Psalms 8 and 139, listing those qualities that seem to exalt man as a marvelous creation. Invite them to work in small groups, recording their answers on newsprint. After a few minutes, have groups share their lists.

Ask: • **What passages in Psalm 8 seem to demonstrate a healthy and biblical balance between recognition of man as important, but not the center of the universe?** • **Is there a difference between self-love and self-centeredness?**

• **In what sense do the following two passages teach the appropriateness of self-love for a Christian?** Mark 12:28-34; Ephesians 5:28-30. • **Is it possible to love someone else in a healthy way if you do not love yourself?**

Self-disparagement is a false substitute for humility. Ask someone in the group to read the two quotes in the chapter from *Screwtape Letters* by C. S. Lewis and the quote from psychologist Karen Horney. Ask: • **Are there other ways that self-disparagement can be selfish and self-centered?**

To conclude this section on self-disparagement read the following excerpt from Frederick Buechner's book, *Wishful Thinking*, in which the facade of self-disparagement masquerades as humility:

Humility is often confused with the gentlemanly self-depreciation of saying you're not much of [an athlete] when you know perfectly well you are. Conscious or otherwise, this kind of humility is a form of gamemanship.

If you really aren't much of [an athlete] you're apt to be proud of yourself for admitting it so humbly. This kind of humility is a low form of comedy.

True humility doesn't consist of thinking ill of yourself but of not thinking of yourself much differently from the way you're apt to think of anybody else. It is the capacity for being no more and no less pleased when you play . . . well than when your opponents do" (Harper & Row, p. 40).

5. **Self-actualization.** This philosophy says, "Accept yourself, express yourself." • From a biblical standpoint, what is good and what is bad about this way of thinking? The book in which this philosophy was most widely espoused was, *I'm OK, You're OK* by Thomas Harris. Ask: • **If you were going to select another title for the book, using the same I'm _____, You're _____ formula, how would you retitle the book so that it more accurately reflects biblical truth?**

6. **Self-surrender.** Read Galatians 2:20. Now, ask someone to demonstrate self-surrender, using the hand and glove again. There are several ways that this might be done. One helpful way is to explain again that the hand is the self and the glove is one's life, but now add that the muscles and blood and arm that controls the hand are representative of Christ. The hand has been "crucified," nevertheless it still lives, but the life it now lives in the flesh, it lives by the life of the Son of God.

7. Tell the class to think of the four areas of discussion as different colors. Self-disparagement is represented by blue (depressed, feeling blue, etc.). Self-extinction is represented by black (nothingness, emptiness). Self-actualization is represented by green (go, accept, express). Surrender is represented by white. **Which color or colors best represent your life?**

8. You read some of the Screwtape strategy earlier in this study. Ask your group members to write a letter from Screwtape to his apprentice Wormwood about how he could use one of these areas to really stop your progress in the Christian life. Have class members read their letters. They should begin as the other Screwtape letters, "My dear Wormwood. . . ."

9. Exhibiting MTM-8 as a quick review, ask class members if the verse they memorized as being special from Psalm 139 especially applies to any of the four ways of dealing with the self. Have them share their answers.

10. Close the session in prayer by having someone read the short prayer at the end of chapter 10.

ASSIGNMENT

1. In your journal this week, write a letter to God in which you explain to Him the toughest area of your life to surrender fully to Him. Explain why. If there has been a crisis moment of surrender in your life, write a brief account of that also.

2. Read chapter 11 in the text.

The Ultimate Crisis of Life / *Text, Chapter 11*

SESSION GOALS
1. To continue discussion of self-surrender.
2. To clarify the three facets of the ego.
3. To see that self-surrender involves both a crisis and a process.

PREPARATION
1. Your discussion will take up where last week's ended. That being the case, it may be helpful to review chapter 10 before you prepare for chapter 11. Bring MTM-8 to this session so that it is available for quick review.
2. You will find helpful material for this week's lesson in the widely known booklet, *My Heart Christ's Home,* by Robert Boyd Munger (Inter-Varsity Press, 1954). This booklet helps people to inventory their own lives for unsurrendered areas. In chapter 11, Dr. Seamands uses an illustration that draws from the idea upon which this book is based—that the believer's heart is Christ's home.
3. Have MTM-9 available as well as a chalkboard and chalk or newsprint and markers for use of VS-10 and VS-11. Write out Galatians 2:20 on a sheet of newsprint, or on a transparency for overhead projection. Use a version that will be understandable by your group.

PRESENTATION
1. As group members arrive this week, have Galatians 2:20 displayed prominently. Begin by showing MTM-8 and reading the following lines from a hymn:
"Oh to be nothing, nothing/Only to lie at His feet,/A broken and emptied vessel/For the Master's use made meet."
Ask: • **Which idea of surrender in MTM-8 seems to underlie this hymn?** • **Is it biblical?** • **Is it healthy?** • **Why or why not?**
2. Give members 10 minutes to read the booklet, *My Heart Christ's Home.* When they finish, they should try to pinpoint the room(s) in which they are most reluctant to invite Christ to make "His home." Spend some time identifying areas in which they have a need of surrendering. You will have to set the pace here for honesty and vulnerability.
3. Say, "There is a point in the Christian life at which place we make a decision of ultimate surrender." Ask for some synonyms of the word "ultimate." Dr. Seamands writes that we must see the difference between Jesus' invitations to "Come unto Me" and "Come after Me." • **How would you describe the difference between these two commands in terms of the booklet we've just read?**
4. Ask them to read Galatians 2:20 silently, then as a group. **Here is a**

verse about self-surrender, but how many first person pronouns do we see? (Eight) Using different color pens, circle all eight instances.

Using VS-10, ask the group to draw either from the verse or from the text to describe each facet of the ego we observe in this verse. As you mention each of the three facets of the ego, go back to your "chart" of Galatians 2:20 and underline the appropriate "I" you're referring to.

5. Dr. Seamands talks about the crucifixion of self as a "Custer's last stand" of sorts, because it is such a grueling and decisive fight. The death of this first facet of the ego, this ultimate crisis of self-surrender is not always, or even usually, a quick shoot-out. It may take a long time to travel from conversion to self-surrender.

Using MTM-9 and *My Heart Christ's Home*, ask group members to suggest various stages along the way from conversion to surrender. In Mark 8:34, we see the decisive act of giving up rights and taking up a cross, but that momentary decision is realized by the process of following—an ongoing process. "Self-surrender is both a definite crisis and a never-ending process" (*Text*).

6. • **What is the difference between a crisis and a process?** • **How is this difference visible in the life of Paul?** For clues here, have some people in the group read Acts 26:9-19 and have the others read Philippians 3:4-16.

VS-10
Draw the various facts of the ego.

Fallen Ego	Selfhood Ego	Christ-Centered Ego
needs crucifixion self-centered prideful	survives self-crucifixion indestructible eternal needs liberation	Christ-filled Christ-possessed

VS-11
Real surrender means giving God the options.

Self-surrender	Self-surrender
Dear Lord, Give me this... Give me that... I want this... Give me the other... "...Lord I surrender. Take my life and let it be...." Name _____	Dear Lord, Name _____

• **When Paul became obedient to that heavenly vision on the Damascus Road, did that mean the end of spiritual struggle for him?** Have different group members read in order the following verses: 1 Corinthians 15:9; Ephesians 3:8; 1 Timothy 1:15. The more mature Paul became in the faith, the more surrendered he became, for he became aware of new areas to surrender.

"You can only surrender to God that which you first acknowledge for yourself. You can surrender your willingness to God, you can make a total surrender of your right to yourself, you can make a full commitment to surrender. But you won't actually be surrendering anything specific until you face some particular issue of the will in a real life situation" (*Text*).

• **How does Jesus' episode in the Garden of Gethsemane demonstrate this idea?** This is a good place to share the proverb quoted by Dr. Seamands: "Your will can go ahead by express, but sometimes your emotions travel by slow freight."

7. Go back now to Philippians 3:4-16 and read through the passage again. See if the group can identify the crisis and the process of Paul's spiritual odyssey. It may be helpful to do this referring again to MTM-9.

8. Christ's surrender, or emptying of Himself, had to be based on His willingness to give up reputation for the sake of obedience. See Philippians 2:6-7. Dr. Seamands admits that this had been the stumblingblock in his own course of surrender. This is, in essence, the same testimony Paul gave in Philippians 3:4-16. • **Why is it that we struggle so much with the idea of continual surrender even after we've become Christians?** • **Is it reputation, misunderstanding, or some other reason?**

9. Dr. Seamands gives two pictures of self-surrender. Using VS-11, ask:
• **Which picture describes you?**

10. Referring one last time to MTM-9, ask group members to write down a few of the points in their own spiritual walks on the way from "here" to "there." • **Where are you now?** • **What is blocking the way?**

11. In closing, ask them to read (silently) the letter they wrote to God as a part of the homework assignment. Then, invite them to pray in unison the hymn which closes the chapter.

ASSIGNMENT

1. Ask four people to pinpoint, as specifically as possible, the major person or event that influenced them to be who they are right now. Jot down these responses and bring them to the next session.

2. Read the last chapter of the book.

Reprogramming Grace / Text, Chapter 12

SESSION GOALS
1. To review the basic thesis of the book, and recognize that these various areas of life are identified so that we can *katargeo* them.
2. To identify the three basic processes that must take place in order for someone to come into genuine wholeness.
3. To examine some of the "flags" that we fly in our daily lives, and see where the healing power of God needs to be applied.

PREPARATION
1. Bring enough sheets of white paper and colored pencils for those in your group to complete the assignment under Presentation 5. You will want at least three to four colored pencils per person.
2. Write the following role play suggestions on pieces of paper for distribution during the session. Members will be observing ways in which God enables believers to deal with the three major areas of fear.

• **Role play situation 1:** Mary has been a good mother and wife for the seven years that she and John have been married. But recently, she finds herself becoming more and more impatient with the three children. Her oldest son of six years has especially been unruly in recent weeks. John has been very busy with work and is out of town a good bit. His absence has taken a toll on the family, and even though it is temporary, it is beginning to wear on Mary and show in the kids' behavior.

Last Thursday was one of those long, hot days that mothers have nightmares about—the four year old daughter fell off her bike and sprained a wrist, and the refrigerator went on the blink. When Mary had just about had it, six-year old Johnny started picking on two-year old Timmy. In a moment of anger like she hadn't really felt before with the kids, she screamed at Johnny and told him to get out of her sight, that she didn't want to see him for a while. This flash of rage was not typical of Mary, and she could see that she had hurt Johnny deeply. She apologized to him, but has felt more and more guilty, more and more inadequate as a mother.

Now she comes to Sue, her neighbor and friend, because she wonders if she's an abusive mother. She's feeling guilty about letting John down. She feels that God is very disappointed because she isn't the mother she should be. All of this is beginning to deeply affect her relationship with the Lord, her husband, and her children. Sue uses Genesis 3:8-10 and 2 Timothy 1:7 to encourage her that she is unconditionally accepted by God in His love.

• **Role play situation 2:** Joe is 28 years old and unmarried. That never really bothered him until recently when his best friend got married. Joe is well-liked and admired by people at his church, but recently, some of his own doubts about himself have caused him to withdraw from in-depth social involvement. His withdrawal has brought him to distrust himself even more, since now he cannot reassure himself by thinking of the positive friendships he has. He begins to wonder if somehow his being unmarried at 28 is an indication of something wrong in his life.

Two days ago, Bob called Joe and asked him to seriously think about teaching the College/Career Sunday School class at church. Three months ago, Joe would have charged into the project with enthusiasm. But, lately, as he has been struggling with some of these self-doubts, he has been wondering about his ability, let alone his "right," to be leading a group of people. His inclination is to teach the class, but he is afraid he will "blow it" and thereby substantiate all he has thought about himself. He shares his concerns with Bob who tries to reassure him by referring to Jesus' parable in Matthew 25:14-30; to 1 Thessalonians 5:23, and Proverbs 16:3.

• **Role play situation 3:** Use the episode of Kathy that Dr. Seamands recounts in this chapter. Have one person play the part of Kathy, and another play the role of Sharon, a friend to whom Kathy comes with her concerns. The conversation takes place just a week before Kathy is to be married. Sharon tries to assure Kathy that she will be more than adequate as wife and lover.

3. Prepare MTM-10 and VS-12. Bring MTM-1 to class.

PRESENTATION

1. Open this session by asking people to share some of the responses they received in answer to the question they were to have asked three or four people. • **Did you find that people were more affected by a positive event or relationship in their past or by a negative event or relationship?**

2. Showing MTM-10, remind the group of Dr. Seamands' remark: "Our adult lives are deeply rooted in our childhood/teenage years and deeply affected by them" (*Text*). You may want to explain MTM-10 a little further by showing the relationship between roots of the past and fruits of the present. But, move on to display MTM-1 and ask: • **What is the connection between what we just observed in the root/fruit diagram, and what we have been talking about during this course?**

3. Read from the book the quote from the *Sports Illustrated* article. Ask:

VS-12
Use to illustrate our needs for forgiveness, healing, and surrender.

42

• **How much truth is there in this statement?** • **How much of our past can we really leave behind?** • **If there is truth to this statement, then isn't it a bit unfair for God to judge us for wrongdoing when it may well be something we were programmed for many years ago?** Refer to the testimony of the converted convict and the news article about the malparenting suit.

4. There are three experiences necessary for a person to come into wholeness: forgiveness, healing, and surrender. Using VS-12, discuss these.

• **Forgiveness.** "The first step toward Christian adulthood is to be done with any subtle form of inner penance and self-condemnation for already forgiven and forgotten sins. The guilty self needs to become the forgiven self" (*Text*). • **What are some of the ways we attempt to deal with guilt other than by the proper means of nailing it to the cross of Jesus?** Sometimes we "put it into a bag and dump it onto someone else." • **What are some ways that we do this?**

• **Healing:** One of the ways that this reprogramming takes place is by a change in our predispositions. To make it easier for us to talk about these predispositions, Dr. Seamands uses the analogy of flags that we raise. Be sure everyone understands the meaning of the term.

a. Red Flag of Resentment. Ask them to share some situations that make them see red. (You may want to tell something from your life first.)

b. Yellow Flags of Fear. These fears are based on a lack of acceptance, a lack of usefulness, and fears of inadequacy. Use the role plays which were prepared earlier to demonstrate ways that God's Word can help us to reprogram some of this fear-filled thinking.

Choose two people to act out the roles for each situation. Have one of the persons read the role descriptions out loud for everyone, and then have the two play out the roles. Take a moment after each role play to "debrief" by asking questions like: • **What was his/her real problem here?** • **What kind of feelings did we observe here?** • **How might these verses have been applied differently to help the person who was hurting?** • **What other help would you suggest?**

c. Black Flags of Abuse. Have someone read from the text the account of the woman who was once a lesbian, or the story of Irene.

• **Surrender:** This has been discussed at length in the last two lessons, so it needs little explanation. Ask someone to read 2 Corinthians 10:4-5 where Paul talks about this reprogramming process of surrender. In the healing process, the computer receives a new program, but in the surrender experience, the computer receives a new programmer altogether. For further illustration, show and explain the Christian flag.

5. Ask group members to design a flag that more or less describes what they feel is the current status of their relationship with the Lord. You provide the materials described earlier and give them several minutes. Instruct them to feel free to use any of the flags already mentioned or to add some of their own, or to combine different flags. Ask volunteers to explain their flags to the group.

6. Invite the group to pray together in closing, participating this week by praying for someone else in the group, perhaps on the basis of what they shared about themselves when explaining their flag.

ASSIGNMENT
Write a letter to yourself about the most memorable aspects of these sessions. Include what gains you want to incorporate into your life.

Review

SESSION GOALS
1. To summarize the essential idea of "putting away childish things."
2. To enable group members to move beyond hearing to doing.

PREPARATION
1. Mentally review the sessions you have had with this group of people. Which ideas and topics seemed to arouse the most interest? Where did there seem to be the greatest amount of confusion? As you ponder these questions, make a note to emphasize these ideas as you review.
2. Before your group members arrive this week, write out 1 Corinthians 13:11 on a large sheet of newsprint or on an overhead transparency. Have this displayed as people enter the room for this session.

PRESENTATION
1. Begin this week by reading together 1 Corinthians 13:11. Using this as your springboard, refer to the working thesis throughout this course by displaying MTM-1.
2. While displaying MTM-10, place an empty transparency over your viewing screen (if you are using an overhead projector), or have MTM-10 displayed in such a way that you can still write on it. Recall Dr. Seamands' observation that "our adult lives are deeply rooted in our childhood and teenage years." Begin your review by working your way through the book, showing the correlation between various roots and various fruits. The method for this will be for you to draw in the root area a specific phenomena of childhood mentioned by Dr. Seamands. Then, ask the group what sort of fruit this childish thinking or behavior will yield in adulthood if it isn't put away. For example, you will label one of the roots: "Brave boys don't cry—foolish childhood mottoes." Then, group members will respond by answering that this type of thinking leads adult Christians to believe that they should never really express intense feelings, or even have them at all.
3. Give the class a chance to reflect on the impact of the course in their own lives. Let volunteers read the letters they have written to themselves.
4. Spend time in prayer together in small groups, praying for one another on the basis of what each has written in the letter to himself.
5. Close the session by reading 1 Corinthians 13:8-13. As you read the passage, insert the plural "we" in each place Paul has used the singular "I."